AUTHORS

ELAINE MEI AOKI

VIRGINIA A. ARNOLD

JAMES FLOOD

JAMES V. HOFFMAN

DIANE LAPP

MIRIAM MARTINEZ

ANNEMARIE SULLIVAN
PALINCSAR

MICHAEL PRIESTLEY

NANCY ROSER

CARL B. SMITH

WILLIAM H. TEALE

JOSEFINA VILLAMIL
TINAJERO

ARNOLD W. WEBB

PEGGY E. WILLIAMS

KAREN D. WOOD

MACMILLAN/McGRAW-HILL SCHOOL PUBLISHING COMPANY

NEW YORK CHICAGO COLUMBUS

AUTHORS, CONSULTANTS, AND REVIEWERS

WRITE IDEA! Authors

Elaine Mei Aoki, James Flood, James V. Hoffman, Diane Lapp, Ana Huerta Macias, Miriam Martinez, Ann McCallum, Michael Priestley, Nancy Roser, Carl B. Smith, William Strong, William H. Teale, Charles Temple, Josefina Villamil Tinajero, Arnold W. Webb, Peggy E. Williams

The approach to writing in Macmillan/McGraw-Hill Reading/Language Arts is based on the strategies and approaches to composition and conventions of language in Macmillan/McGraw-Hill's writing-centered language arts program, WRITE IDEA!

Multicultural and Educational Consultants

Alma Flor Ada, Yvonne Beamer, Joyce Buckner, Helen Gillotte, Cheryl Hudson, Narcita Medina, Lorraine Monroe, James R. Murphy, Sylvia Peña, Joseph B. Rubin, Ramon Santiago, Cliff Trafzer, Hai Tran, Esther Lee Yao

Literature Consultants

Ashley Bryan, Joan I. Glazer, Paul Janeczko, Margaret H. Lippert

International Consultants

Edward B. Adams, Barbara Johnson, Raymond L. Marshall

Music and Audio Consultants

John Farrell, Marilyn C. Davidson, Vincent Lawrence, Sarah Pirtle, Susan R. Snyder, Rick and Deborah Witkowski

Teacher Reviewers

Terry Baker, Jane Bauer, James Bedi, Nora Bickel, Vernell Bowen, Donald Cason, Jean Chaney, Carolyn Clark, Alan Cox, Kathryn DesCarpentrie, Carol L. Ellis, Roberta Gale, Brenda Huffman, Erma Inscore, Sharon Kidwell, Elizabeth Love, Isabel Marcus, Elaine McCraney, Michelle Moraros, Earlene Parr, Dr. Richard Potts, Jeanette Pulliam, Michael Rubin, Henrietta Sakamaki, Kathleen Cultron Sanders, Belinda Snow, Dr. Jayne Steubing, Margaret Mary Sulentic, Barbara Tate, Seretta Vincent, Willard Waite, Barbara Wilson, Veronica York

ACKNOWLEDGMENTS

The publisher gratefully acknowledges permission to reprint the following copyrighted material:

"A Birthday Basket for Tia" from A BIRTHDAY BASKET FOR TIA by Pat Mora. Illustrations by Cecily Lang. Text copyright © 1992 by Pat Mora. Illustrations copyright © 1992 by Cecily Lang. Reprinted with permission from Macmillan Publishing Company, a division of Macmillan, Inc.

"A Letter to Amy" is the entire work of A LETTER TO AMY by Ezra Jack Keats. Copyright © 1968 by Ezra Jack Keats. Reprinted by permission of HarperCollins Publishers.

"As the sun came up, a ball of red...." from CHINESE MOTHER GOOSE RHYMES selected and edited by Robert Wyndham. Copyright © 1968 by Robert Wyndham. Reprinted and recorded by permission of Philomel Books.

"Baby Rattlesnake" told by Te Ata; Adapted by Lynn Moroney. Text copyright © 1989 by Lynn Moroney. Illustrations (including cover art) copyright © 1989 by Veg Reisberg. Reprinted by permission of GRM Associates, Inc., agents for Children's Book Press.

"Celebration" by Alonzo Lopez from WHISPERING WIND by Terry Allen. Copyright © 1972 by the Institute of American Indian Arts. Used by permission of Doubleday, a division of Bantam Doubleday Dell Publishing Group, Inc.

"Eat Up, Gemma" written by Sarah Hayes, illustrated by Jan Ormerod. Text copyright © 1988 by Sarah Hayes. Illustrations copyright © 1988 by Jan Ormerod. Reprinted by permission of Lothrop, Lee & Shepard Books, a division of William Morrow and Company, Inc., Publishers, New York.

Excerpt from "Parades" from MY DADDY IS A COOL DUDE AND OTHER POEMS by Karama Fufuka. Copyright © 1975 by Karama Fufuka. Used by permission of Dial Books for Young Readers, a division of Penguin Books USA Inc.

"Follow the Leader" from THE WIZARD IN THE WELL by Harry Behn. Copyright © 1956 by Harry Behn. © renewed 1984 Alice Behn Goebel, Pamela Behn Adam, Peter Behn and Prescott Behn. Used by permission of Marian Reiner.

"Fortunately" is from FORTUNATELY by Remy Charlip. Copyright © 1980 by Remy Charlip. Reprinted with permission from Four Winds Press, an imprint of Macmillan Publishing Company.

"Guinea Pigs Don't Read Books" by Colleen Stanley Bare. Copyright © 1985 by Colleen Stanley Bare for text. Copyright © 1985 by Colleen Stanley Bare for photographs. Used by permission of Cobblehill Books, an affiliate of Dutton Children's Books, a division of Penguin USA Inc.

"Happy Birthday to Me" from CATCH A LITTLE RHYME by Eve Merriam. Copyright © 1966 by Eve Merriam. Reprinted by permission of Marian Reiner for the author.

"Henry and Mudge in Puddle Trouble" by Cynthia Rylant. Illustrated by Suçie Stevenson. Text and art of "Puddle Trouble." Text copyright © 1987 by Cynthia Rylant. Illustrations copyright © 1987 by Suçie Stevenson.

(Continued on page 288)

1995 Printing

Macmillan/McGraw-Hill School Division
10 Union Square East
New York, New York 10003

Printed in the United States of America
ISBN 0-02-178755-7 / 1, L.5
    5 6 7 8 9 VHJ 99 98 97 96 95 94

To Jonathan Stribling-Uss
and the first graders
who taught me about
THE VERY THING—
the joyful discovery of reading.

Anne Stribling

To our families and friends,
whose love and support are
the _very_ _thing_ we need
to fill our baskets.

Alice Dickstein

Being Family, Being Friends

You're Invited!

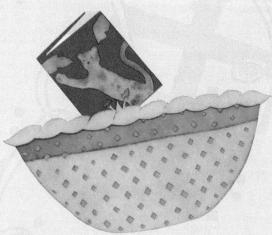

6

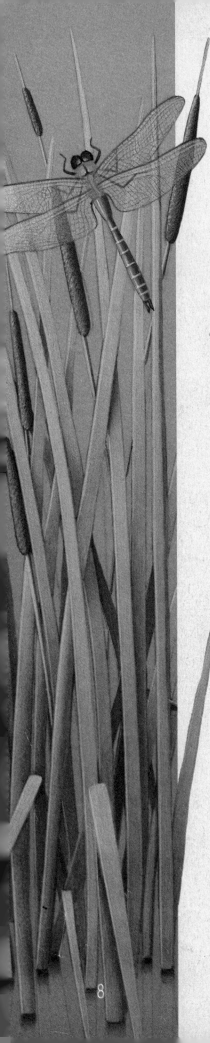
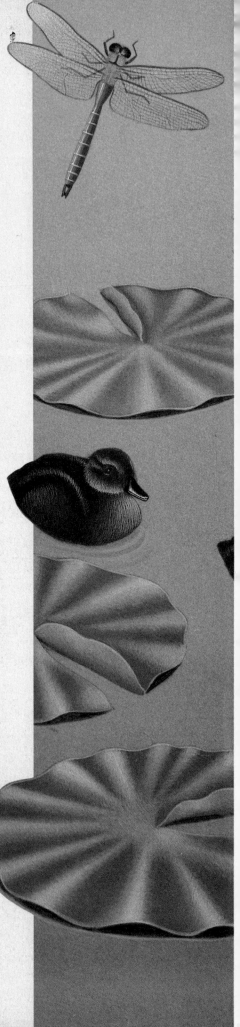

CONTENTS

Being FAMILY, Being FRIENDS

Something for everyone,
that's when a family's fun.
There's lots of surprises,
with different sizes
and shapes to a family.
Something for sharing there,
with people caring there.
It's a door you can go in,
a place you can grow in.
It's anything you need it to be.

CAROL HALL
from *Something for Everyone*

10

MEET CYNTHIA RYLANT

Cynthia Rylant has written many books about Henry and Mudge. She says that Henry is like her son, Nate. "Nate thought huge puddles were wonderful when he was seven years old. Mudge is like a real dog we had who weighed 200 pounds."

Ms. Rylant says she would like to be more like Henry's father. "I make Henry's father do all the goofy things I'd like to do," she says.

MEET SUÇIE STEVENSON

Henry and Mudge in Puddle Trouble was fun for Suçie Stevenson to illustrate. She says, "I've always lived near water. I've seen how much fun dogs have in water. Puddles are fun for people, too. You play in them. You get earthworms out of them."

Henry and Mudge
in
Puddle Trouble

by Cynthia Rylant
illustrated by Suçie Stevenson

In April
it rained
day after day
after day
after day.

Henry was getting bored.
Mudge was chewing up
everything in the house.
So Henry said,
"Let's play outside anyway."

He put on his raincoat
and sneakers
and went outside with Mudge.
Henry forgot to ask his father
if it was all right.

When Mudge stepped
into the wet grass,
he lifted his paws
and shook them.

"Too bad you don't
have sneakers," Henry said.
And he walked in a circle
around Mudge.
Squish, squish, squish, squish.

Mudge listened
and looked at Henry.
Then he got closer
to Henry
and wagged his tail
and shook the water from
his big wet furry body
all over Henry.

Henry wiped the water
from his face.
"Aw, Mudge," he said.

The two of them
went walking.
And down the road
they found a big puddle.
A giant puddle.
A lake puddle.
An ocean puddle.
And Henry said, "Wow!"

He started running.
Mudge got there first.
SPLASH!
Muddy water all over Mudge.

SPLASH!

Muddy water all over Henry.

It was the biggest,

deepest puddle

they had ever seen.

And they loved it.

When Henry's father
called for Henry
and didn't find him,
he went outside.
He looked down the road.
SPLASH! he heard.
He put on his raincoat
and went walking.

SPLASH! he saw.
Henry's father saw Mudge,
with a muddy face
and muddy tail
and muddy in between.

Henry's father saw Henry,
with a muddy face
and muddy sneakers
and muddy in between.
And he yelled, *"Henry!"*
No more splashes.
Just a boy and a dog,
dripping.

"Hi, Dad," Henry said,
with a little smile.
Mudge wagged his tail.

"Henry, you know
you should have asked me first,"
Henry's father said.

"I know," said Henry.

"I am surprised at you,"
Henry's father said.

"I'm sorry," said Henry.

"I don't know what to do
with you," Henry's father said.

Henry looked sad.
Then Mudge wagged his tail,
licked Henry's hand,
and shook the water
from his big wet furry body
all over Henry and Henry's father.

"Mudge!" Henry yelled.

Henry's father stood there
with a muddy face
and muddy shoes
and muddy in between.
He looked at Mudge,
he looked at Henry,
he looked at the big puddle.

Then he smiled.
"Wow," he said.
And he jumped in.

He splashed water on Mudge.
He splashed water on Henry.
He said, "Next time, ask me along!"

Henry said, "Sure, Dad."
And Henry splashed him back.

IT'S RA

Why did the girl wear her rain boots in the pet store?

She didn't want to get her feet wet in the poodles.

What kind of dog never cools off in a summer shower?

A hot dog.

What did the dog say to the flea?

Don't bug me.

When is it not safe to walk in the rain?

When it is raining cats and dogs.

CATS A
DON'T STEP IN

...INING

How did the kitten know it was going to rain?

It listened to the furcast.

What kind of dog always knows when the first raindrop begins to fall?

A watchdog.

What is a cat's favorite winter sport?

Mice-skating.

...ND DOGS
THE POODLES!

As the sun came up, a ball of red,

I followed my friend wherever he led.

He thought his fast horse would leave me behind,

But I rode a dragon as swift as the wind!

from **The Chinese Mother Goose**

EAT UP, GEMMA

Written by Sarah Hayes

Illustrated by Jan Ormerod

One morning we woke up late.
I couldn't find my shoes
and Gemma wouldn't eat her breakfast.

"Eat up, Gemma," said Mom,
but Gemma threw her breakfast on the floor.

37

Later on we went to the market.
Mom bought a bag of apples
and some bananas.
The man at the fruit stand
gave me a bunch of grapes.
He gave some to Gemma, too.

"Eat up, Gemma," said the man,
but Gemma pulled the
grapes off one by one
and squashed them.

When we got home
Grandma had made dinner.
"Nice and spicy," Dad said,
"just how I like it."
It was nice and spicy all right.
I drank three glasses of water.

"Eat up, Gemma," said Grandma.

Gemma banged her spoon on the table
and shouted.
But she didn't eat a thing.

42

The next day was Saturday
and Dad took us to the park.
We had chocolate cookies for a treat.
I ate two and then another two.

"Eat up, Gemma," said Dad.

But Gemma didn't eat her cookie.
She just licked off all the chocolate
and gave the rest to the birds.

In the evening our friends
were having a party.

"Eat up, everyone," said our friends.

And we did, all except Gemma.
She sat on Grandma's knee
and gave her dinner to the dog
when Grandma wasn't looking.

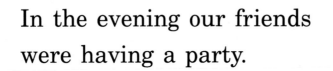

45

After the party my friend came to stay
and we had a midnight feast.
Gemma didn't have any.
She was too tired.

In the morning we made Gemma a feast.

"Eat up, Gemma," said my friend.

Gemma picked up her toy hammer
and banged her feast to pieces.
My friend thought it was funny,
but Mom and Dad didn't.

Soon it was time for us to put on
our best clothes and go to church.
I sang very loudly.

The lady in front of us
had a hat with fruit on it.
I could see Gemma looking and looking.

When everyone was really quiet
Gemma leaned forward.

"Eat up, Gemma," she said.

Then she tried to pull
a grape off the lady's hat.
She pulled and pulled
and the lady's hat fell off.
Gemma hid her face in Dad's coat.

54

When we got home I had an idea.
I found a plate and a bowl.
I turned the bowl upside down
and put it on the plate.
Then I took a bunch of grapes
and two bananas and put them on the plate.
It looked just like the lady's hat.

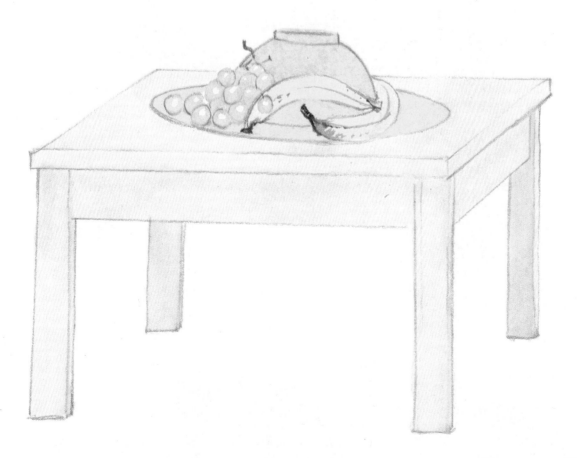

"Eat up, Gemma," I said.

And she did.
She ate all the grapes
and the bananas.
She even tried to
eat the skins.

"Thank goodness for that," said Mom.

"We were getting worried," said Dad.
Grandma smiled at me.
I felt very proud.

"Gemma eat up," said Gemma,
and we all laughed.

Meet Sarah Hayes

Sarah Hayes wrote *Eat Up, Gemma*
because she had noticed something funny
about babies. She says, "It's very odd.
There are times when babies suddenly don't
like food. They might play with it, but
they don't want to eat it!"

Ms. Hayes adds, "Babies are very cuddly
and sweet. But they can make you mad.
Like Gemma's brother, we know they
don't mean to be naughty. And we love
them anyway."

Meet Jan Ormerod

The pictures Jan Ormerod drew in *Eat Up, Gemma* are of a West Indian family now living in England. "These people are friends of mine. My friends acted as models," she says. "They let me draw from their family photographs, too."

Jan Ormerod says, "It was fun to make pictures of things babies do because my little girl was doing those things."

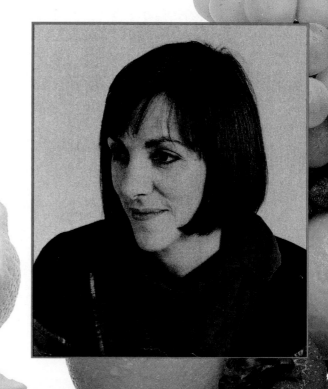

A Country Far Away

by Nigel Gray
illustrated by
Philippe Dupasquier
Orchard Books, 1989

Today I looked at some pictures of
a country far away. I'd like to go
there someday and make a friend.

NEAR AND FAR

Clean Your Room, Harvey Moon!

by Pat Cummings
illustrated by Pat Cummings
Bradbury Press, 1991

Under his desk were some comics
All icky
From something inside
That was dripping and sticky.

Meet

Colleen Stanley Bare

Colleen Stanley Bare has taken pictures of many animals. One day she noticed how many kinds of guinea pigs there are. So she decided to write *Guinea Pigs Don't Read Books*.

Children often ask Ms. Bare, "How do you get a guinea pig?" She tells them, "Lots of pet shops have guinea pigs or you can look in newspapers under 'Pets' and find them advertised for sale."

Ms. Bare says that when she writes she has to pick out the very best words to use. "Each word in this book was crossed out and changed many times. I go over and over the words in my books until I like the way they sound."

Guinea Pigs Don't Read Books

by Colleen Stanley Bare

Guinea pigs don't read books,
count numbers, run computers,

play checkers, or watch TV,
but there are other things they do.

They chew, and chew, and chew.
Foods like apples, celery, carrots,
and if you don't watch out,
they'll chew your toys.

Guinea pigs see well
and stare at you.

They hear well
and listen.

They smell well
and sniff and sniff.

Guinea pigs make sounds.
They growl, grunt, gurgle,
purr, squeal, whistle,
and squeak, squeak, squeak.

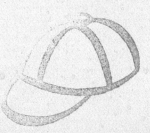

Guinea pigs don't wear hats,
but they do wear fur coats.

Short, soft smooth ones

rough, bristly ones

long, silky ones.

Their coats come in many colors.

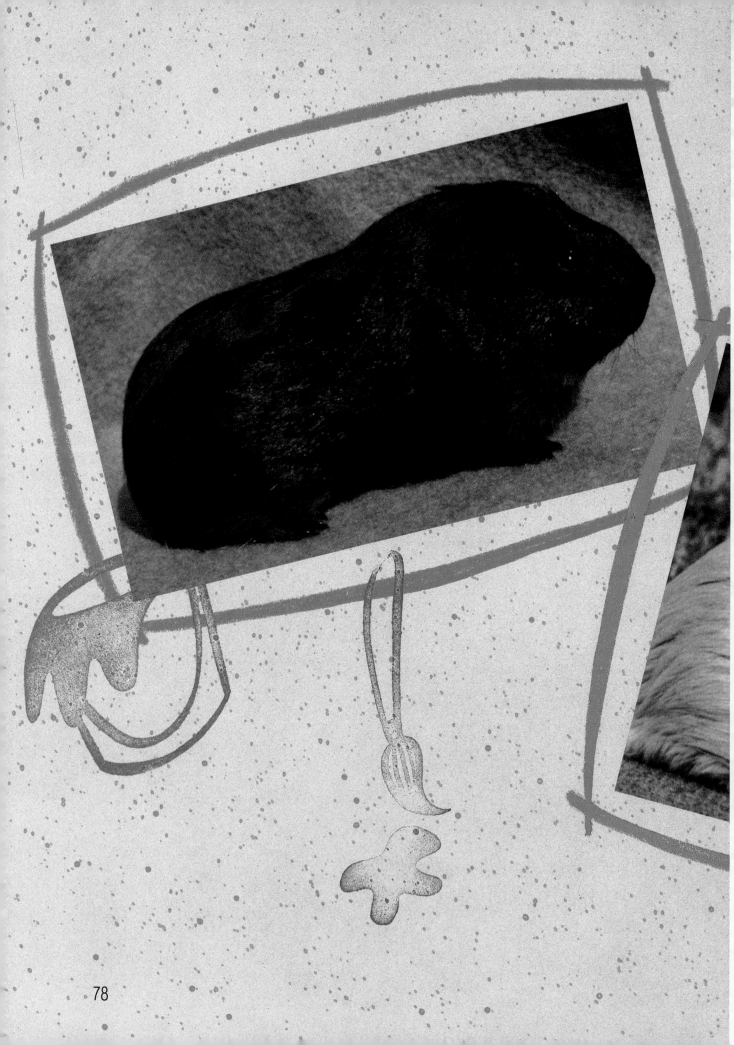

Blue, beige, cream,
red, orange, lilac,
chocolate, white, black.

And in mixtures of colors.

Guinea pigs aren't pigs.
They don't eat like pigs,
walk like pigs, sound like pigs.

Even baby guinea pigs
don't look like baby pigs.

Guinea pigs like to be held and hugged.
They are gentle and calm and lovable.

Guinea pigs may not read books,
but they can be your friends.

Follow the Leader

Follow the leader away in a row,
Into the barn and out we go,
A long slide down the hay,
Splash in a puddle, through a hedge,
And slowly up to the buzzing edge
Of a bees' hive, then run away!
Oh what a wonderful game to play!
Follow the leader on and on,
Around a tree, across a lawn,
Under the sprinkler's drifting spray,
Eat one berry, let two drop,
A somersault and a hippity-hop!
Oh what a wonderful game to play!
All over the farm on a summer day!

Harry Behn

BABY RATTLE

SNAKE

A FOLK TALE TOLD BY TE ATA
AND RETOLD BY LYNN MORONEY
ILLUSTRATED BY MIRA (VEG) REISBERG

Out in the place where the rattlesnakes lived, there was a little baby rattlesnake who cried all the time because he did not have a rattle.

He said to his mother and father, "I don't know why I don't have a rattle. I'm made just like my brother and sister. How can I be a rattlesnake if I don't have a rattle?"

Mother and Father Rattlesnake said, "You are too young to have a rattle. When you get to be as old as your brother and sister, you will have a rattle, too."

But Baby Rattlesnake did not want to
wait. So he just cried and cried. He
shook his tail and when he couldn't
hear a rattle sound, he cried even
louder.

Mother and Father said, "Shhh! Shhh!
Shhhhh!"

Brother and Sister said, "Shhh! Shhh!
Shhhhh!"

But Baby Rattlesnake wouldn't stop crying. He kept the Rattlesnake People awake all night.

The next morning, the Rattlesnake People called a big council. They talked and they talked just like people do, but they couldn't decide how to make that little baby rattlesnake happy. He didn't want anything else but a rattle.

At last one of the elders said, "Go ahead, give him a rattle. He's too young and he'll get into trouble. But let him learn a lesson. I just want to get some sleep."

So they gave Baby Rattlesnake a rattle.

Baby Rattlesnake loved his rattle. He shook his tail and for the first time he heard, "Ch-Ch-Ch! Ch-Ch-Ch!" He was so excited!

He sang a rattle song, "Ch-Ch-Ch! Ch-Ch-Ch!"

He danced a rattle dance, "Ch-Ch-Ch! Ch-Ch-Ch!"

Soon Baby Rattlesnake learned to play tricks with his rattle. He hid in the rocks and when the small animals came by, he darted out rattling, "Ch-Ch-Ch!" "Ch-Ch-Ch!"

ha ha

He made Jack Rabbit jump.
He made Old Man Turtle jump.
He made Prairie Dog jump.

Each time Baby Rattlesnake
laughed and laughed. He thought it
was fun to scare the animal people.

Mother and Father warned Baby Rattlesnake, "You must not use your rattle in such a way."

Big Brother and Big Sister said, "You are not being careful with your rattle."

The Rattlesnake People told Baby Rattlesnake to stop acting so foolish with his rattle.

Baby Rattlesnake did not listen.

One day, Baby Rattlesnake said to his mother and father, "How will I know a chief's daughter when I see her?"

"Well, she's usually very beautiful and walks with her head held high," said Father.

"And she's very neat in her dress," added Mother.

"Why do you want to know?" asked Father.

"Because I want to scare her!" said Baby Rattlesnake. And he started right off down the path before his mother and father could warn him never to do a thing like that.

The little fellow reached the place where the Indians traveled. He curled himself up on a log and he started rattling. "Chh-Chh-Chh!" He was having a wonderful time.

All of a sudden he saw a beautiful maiden coming toward him from a long way off. She walked with her head held high, and she was very neat in her dress.

"Ah," thought Baby Rattlesnake. "She must be the chief's daughter."

Baby Rattlesnake hid in the rocks. He was excited. This was going to be his best trick.

He waited and waited. The chief's daughter came closer and closer. When she was in just the right spot, he darted out of the rocks.

"Ch-Ch-Ch-Ch-Ch!"

Ho!" cried the chief's daughter. She whirled around, stepping on Baby Rattlesnake's rattle and crushing it to pieces.

Baby Rattlesnake looked at his beautiful rattle scattered all over the trail. He didn't know what to do.

He took off for home as fast as he could.

With great sobs, he told Mother and Father what had happened. They wiped his tears and gave him big rattlesnake hugs.

For the rest of that day, Baby Rattlesnake stayed safe and snug, close by his rattlesnake family.

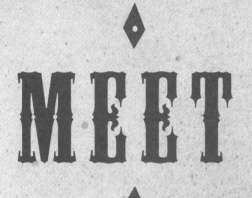

MEET

TE ATA
LYNN MORONEY
MIRA (VEG) REISBERG

TE ATA is a Native American storyteller from Oklahoma. The words in her name are Chickasaw words. They mean "The One Who Brings the Morning."

Te Ata is almost a hundred years old. She learned her first Chickasaw story from her father. Later, Te Ata learned more Native American stories. She traveled to many places telling them, singing Indian songs and saying Indian poems.

LYNN MORONEY is a storyteller from Oklahoma. She asked Te Ata if she could retell the story of Baby Rattlesnake. At first, Te Ata said no. Later, Te Ata heard Ms. Moroney tell some other tales. She was so impressed that she agreed to let Lynn retell Baby Rattlesnake in a book.

MIRA (VEG) REISBERG says, "I can understand Baby Rattlesnake. When I was younger, I threw tantrums when I didn't get what I wanted. Now, if I ever feel like throwing a tantrum, I tell myself not to do a Baby Rattlesnake!"

two friends

lydia and shirley have

two pierced ears and

two bare ones

five pigtails

two pairs of sneakers

two berets

two smiles

one necklace

one bracelet

lots of stripes and

one good friendship

Nikki Giovanni

CONTENTS

124

You're Invited!

126

Parades

I like to see parades
with the marching bands
and big bass drums;
They make me want to dance
and clap my hands.

KARAMA FUFUKA

127

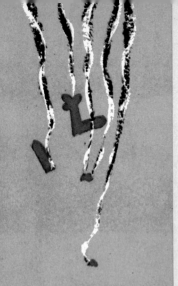

MEET
REMY CHARLIP

Remy Charlip has worked with children as an actor, a dancer, an artist, and a teacher. He has written many children's books.

Before *Fortunately* became a picture book, it was a short play that Mr. Charlip wrote for a children's theater. In the play, two actors stood on each side of the stage and told what happened to Ned.

Mr. Charlip says, "Unfortunately it didn't work well as a play." Then he laughs and adds, "Fortunately it seems to work better as a story."

FORTUNATELY

Written and illustrated by
REMY CHARLIP

Fortunately
one day, Ned got a letter that said,
"Please Come to a Surprise Party."

*But unfortunately
the party was in Florida
and he was in New York.*

Fortunately
a friend loaned him an airplane.

Unfortunately
the motor exploded.

Fortunately
there was a parachute in the airplane.

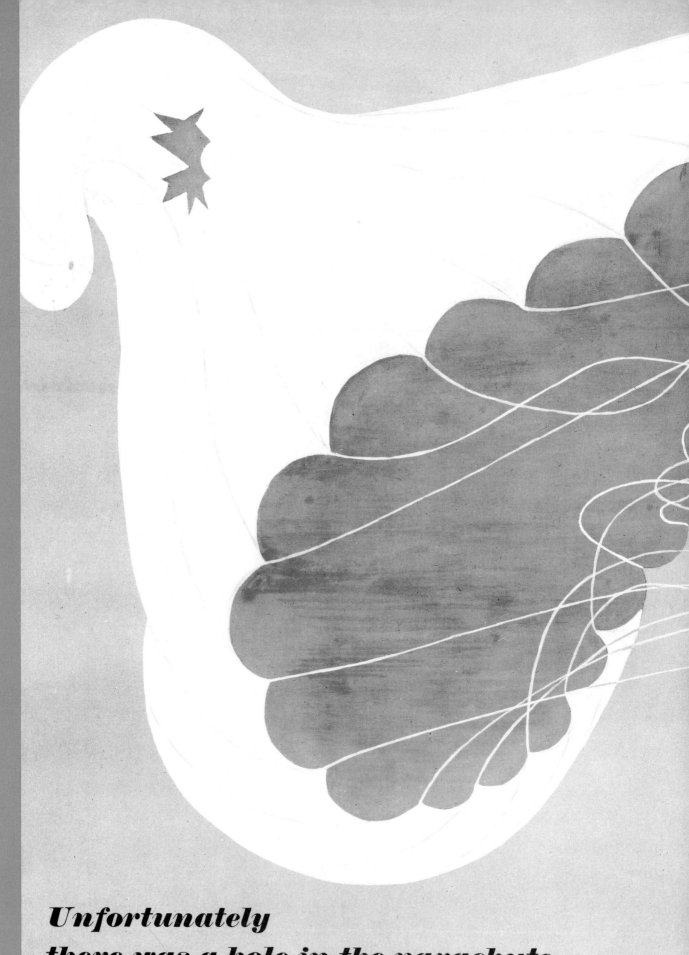

Unfortunately
there was a hole in the parachute.

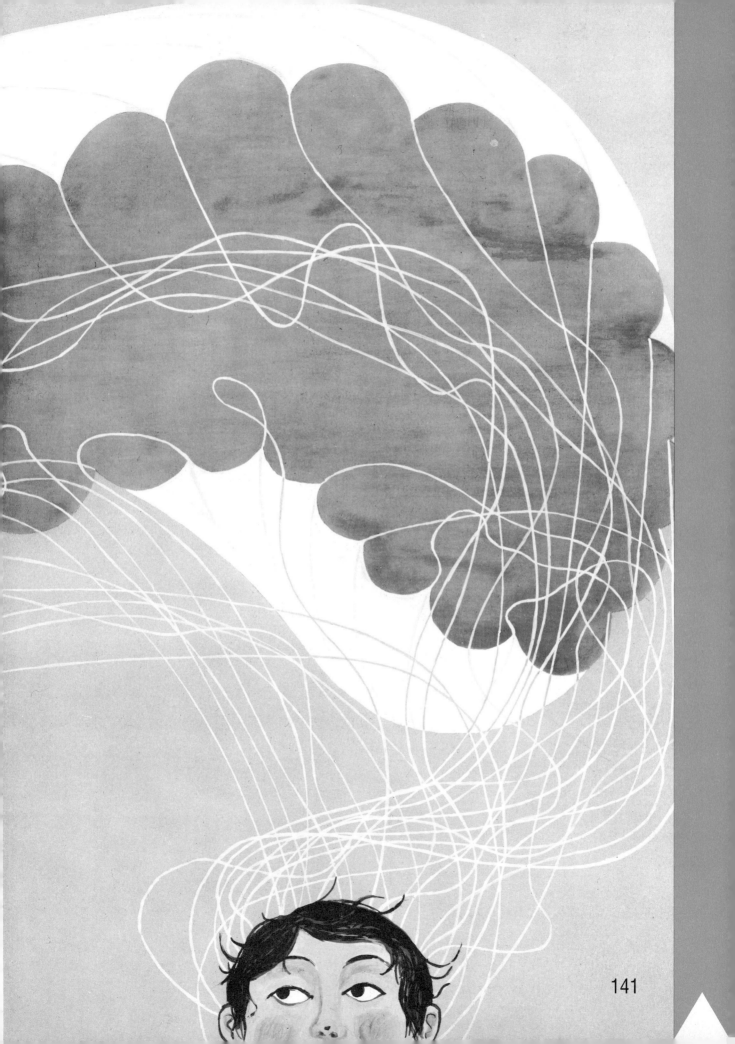

Fortunately
there was a haystack on the ground.

**Unfortunately
there was a pitchfork in the haystack.**

Fortunately
he missed the pitchfork.

Unfortunately
he missed the haystack.

**Fortunately
he landed in water.**

Unfortunately
there were sharks in the water.

Fortunately
he could swim.

Unfortunately
there were tigers on the land.

**Fortunately
he could run.**

Unfortunately
he ran into a deep dark cave.

Fortunately
he could dig.

Unfortunately
he dug himself into a fancy ballroom.

*Fortunately
there was a surprise party going on.
And fortunately
the party was for him,
because fortunately
it was his birthday!*

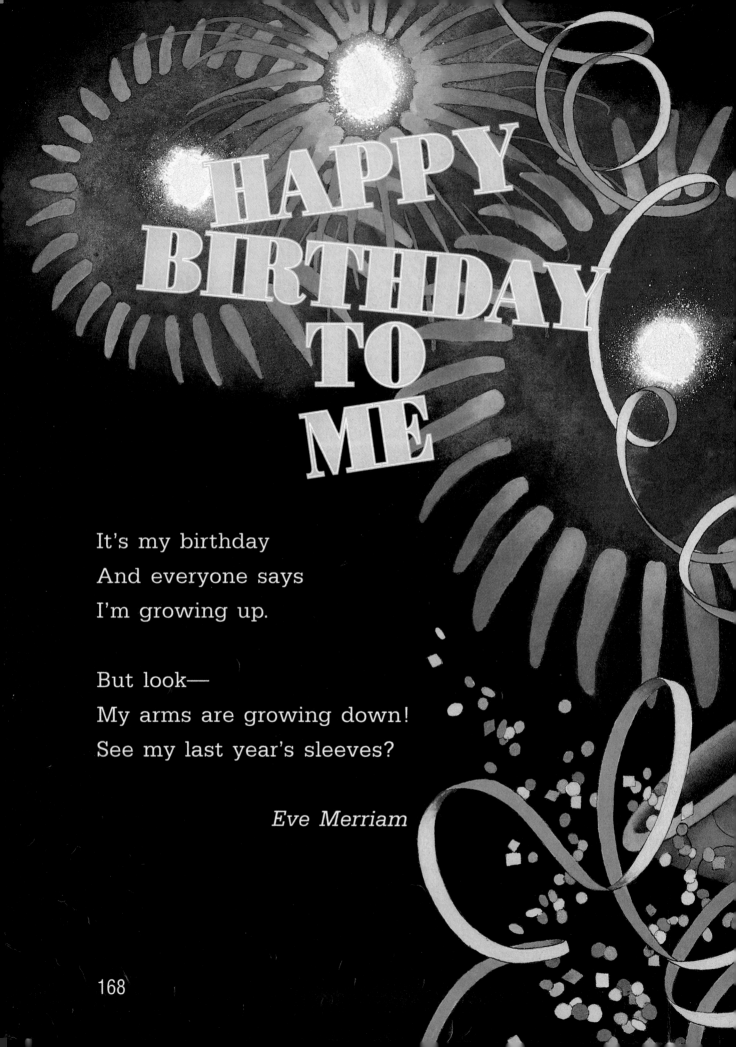

HAPPY BIRTHDAY TO ME

It's my birthday
And everyone says
I'm growing up.

But look—
My arms are growing down!
See my last year's sleeves?

Eve Merriam

MEET PAT MORA

Pat Mora says that children sometimes wonder why some of the words in her stories are Spanish. She tells them, "I want children reading my stories to hear the sounds they would really hear in a Hispanic home. If you came to my house, you would hear my family talking in two kinds of words—English words and Spanish words. The words have different sounds."

She adds, "All homes are alike in some ways, and different in other ways. In *A Birthday Basket for Tía,* one thing that makes Cecilia's home special is that her family speaks two languages. What are some things that make *your* home special?"

A
BIRTHDAY BASKET
FOR TIA

BY PAT MORA
ILLUSTRATED BY CECILY LANG

Today is secret day. I curl my cat into my arms and say, "Ssshh, Chica. Today is secret day. Can you keep our secret, silly cat?"

Today is birthday day. Today is my great-aunt's ninetieth birthday. Ten, twenty, thirty, forty, fifty, sixty, seventy, eighty, ninety. Ninety years old. *¡Noventa años!*

At breakfast Mamá says, "What is today, Cecilia?"

I say, "Secret day. Birthday day."

Mamá is cooking for the surprise party. I smell beans bubbling on the stove. Mamá is cutting fruit, pineapple, watermelon, mangoes. I sit in the backyard and watch Chica chase butterflies. I hear bees bzzzzzzz.

I draw pictures in the sand with a stick. I draw a picture of Tía, my aunt. I say, "Chica, what will we give Tía?"

Chica and I walk around the front yard and the
backyard looking for a good present. We walk
around the house. We look in Mamá's room. We
look in my closet and drawers.

I say, "Chica, shall we give her my little pots, my
piggy bank, my tin fish, my dancing puppet?"

I say, "Mamá, can Chica and I use this basket?"
Mamá asks, "Why, Cecilia?"

"It's a surprise for the surprise party," I answer.

Chica jumps into the basket. "No," I say. "Not you,
silly cat. This is a birthday basket for Tía."

177

I put a book at the bottom of the basket.

When Tía comes to our house, she reads it to me.
It's our favorite book. I sit close to her on the
sofa. I smell her perfume. Sometimes Chica tries
to read with us. She sits on the book. I say, "Silly
cat. Books are not for sitting."

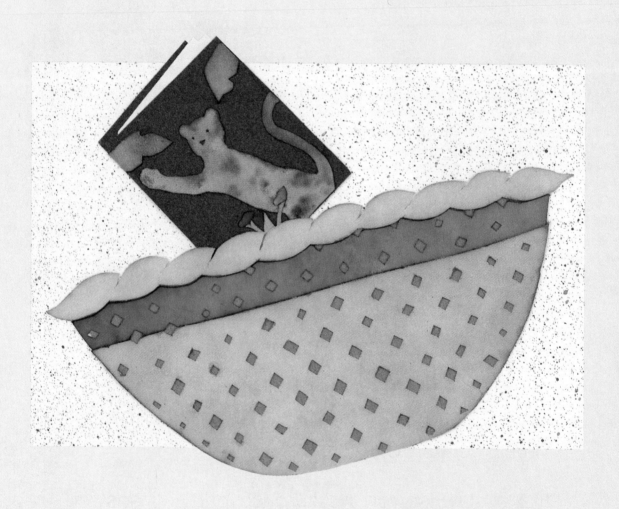

I put Tía's favorite mixing bowl on the book in the basket.

Tía and I like to make *bizcochos,* sugary Mexican cookies for the family.

Tía says, "Cecilia, help me stir the cookie dough." She says, "Cecilia, help me roll the cookie dough."

When we take the warm cookies from the oven, Tía says, "Cecilia, you are a very good cook."

I put a flowerpot in the mixing bowl on the book in the basket.

Tía and I like to grow flowers for the kitchen window. Chica likes to put her face in the flowers. "Silly cat," I say.

I put a teacup in the flowerpot that is in the mixing bowl on the book in the basket.

When I'm sick, my aunt makes me hot mint tea, *hierbabuena*. She brings it to me in bed. She brings me a cookie too.

I put a red ball in the teacup that is in the
flowerpot in the mixing bowl on the book in the
basket.

On warm days Tía sits outside and throws me the
ball. She says, "Cecilia, when I was a little girl in
Mexico, my sisters and I played ball. We all wore
long dresses and had long braids."

Chica and I go outside. I pick flowers to decorate
Tía's basket. On summer days when I am
swinging high up to the sky, Tía collects flowers
for my room.

Mamá calls, "Cecilia, where are you?"

Chica and I run and hide our surprise.

I say, "Mamá, can you find the birthday basket for Tía?"

Mamá looks under the table. She looks in the refrigerator. She looks under my bed. She asks, "Chica, where is the birthday basket?"

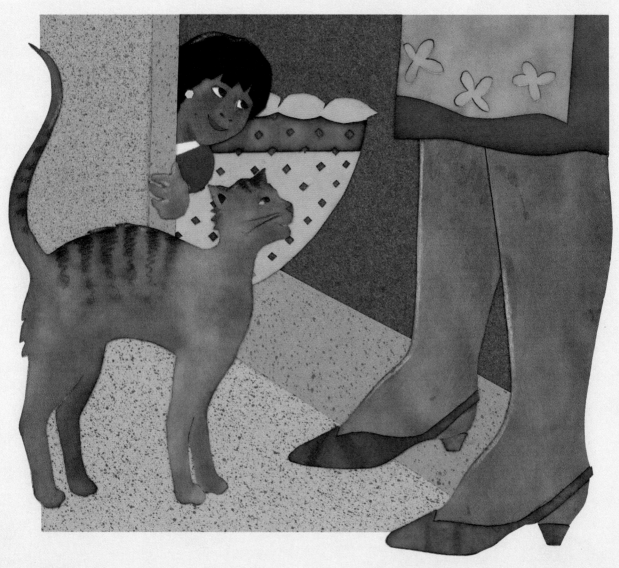

Chica rubs against my closet door. Mamá and I laugh. I show her my surprise.

After my nap, Mamá and I fill a *piñata* with candy. We fill the living room with balloons. I hum, "MMMMM," a little work song like Tía hums when she sets the table or makes my bed. I help Mamá set the table with flowers and tiny cakes.

"Here come the musicians," says Mamá. I open the front door. Our family and friends begin to arrive too.

I curl Chica into my arms. Then Mamá says, "Sshh, here comes Tía."

I rush to open the front door. "Tía! Tía!" I say.

She hugs me and says, "Cecilia, *qué pasa,* what is this?"

193

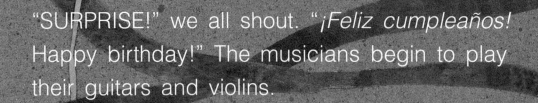

"SURPRISE!" we all shout. "¡Feliz cumpleaños! Happy birthday!" The musicians begin to play their guitars and violins.

194

"Tía! Tía!" I say. "It's secret day, birthday day!
It's your ninetieth birthday surprise party!" Tía
and I start to laugh.

I give her the birthday basket. Everyone gets close to see what's inside. Slowly Tía smells the flowers. She looks at me and smiles.

Then she takes the red ball out of the teacup and the teacup out of the flowerpot. She pretends to take a sip of tea, and we all laugh.

197

Carefully, Tía takes the flowerpot out of the bowl and the bowl off of the book. She doesn't say a word. She just stops and looks at me. Then she takes our favorite book out of the basket.

And guess who jumps into the basket?
(Turn the page.)

Chica.

Everyone laughs.

Then the music starts and my aunt surprises me.
She takes my hands in hers. Without her cane,
she starts to dance with me.

Meet Cecily Lang

Cecily Lang says that watching people helps her be a better artist. She says, "I always peek at people and see how they're feeling by looking at their mouths and their cheeks. I look at their smiles and their frowns."

First, Ms. Lang draws pictures on regular paper. Next, she traces each part of the picture on a special piece of paper and cuts each piece with a sharp knife. Then, she dyes each piece of paper the color she wants. She puts the pieces together like a jigsaw puzzle and holds them together with tape. Then, she glues all the pieces together. Last, she colors the pieces lightly with a pencil.

Invitation

My birthday invitation
has balloons
of red and blue.

It says *come soon*
and *please reply,*

My name is on it too.
It tells the place where we will meet
And shows the time and date.

So *please reply*
And say you'll *come*

to help me celebrate!

Myra Cohn Livingston

203

Ask Mr. Bear

by Marjorie Flack

illustrated by Marjorie Flack

Aladdin, 1986

ASK MR. BEAR
By Marjorie Flack

My Puppy Is Born

by Joanna Cole

photos by Margaret Miller

Morrow, 1991

Mr. Rabbit and

the Lovely Present

by Charlotte Zolotow

illustrated by Maurice Sendak

"Mr. Rabbit," said the little girl, "I want help."

"Help, little girl, I'll give you help if I can," said Mr. Rabbit.

"Mr. Rabbit," said the little girl, "it's about my mother."

"Your mother?" said Mr. Rabbit.

"It's her birthday," said the little girl.

"Happy birthday to her then," said Mr. Rabbit. "What are you giving her?"

"That's just it," said the little girl. "That's why I want help. I have nothing to give her."

"Nothing to give your mother on her birthday?" said Mr. Rabbit. "Little girl, you really do want help."

"I would like to give her something that she likes," said the little girl.

"Something that she likes is a good present," said Mr. Rabbit.

"But what?" said the little girl.

"Yes, what?" said Mr. Rabbit.

"She likes red," said the little girl.

"Red," said Mr. Rabbit. "You can't give her red."

"Something red, maybe," said the little girl.

"Oh, something red," said Mr. Rabbit.

"What is red?" said the little girl.

"Well," said Mr. Rabbit, "there's red underwear."

"No," said the little girl, "I can't give her that."

"There are red roofs," said Mr. Rabbit.

"No, we have a roof," said the little girl.
"I don't want to give her that."

"There are red birds," said Mr. Rabbit, "red cardinals."

"No," said the little girl, "she likes birds in trees."

"There are red fire engines," said Mr. Rabbit.

"No," said the little girl, "she doesn't like fire engines."

"Well," said Mr. Rabbit, "there are apples."

"Good," said the little girl. "That's good. She likes apples. But I need something else."

"What else does she like?" said Mr. Rabbit.

"Well, she likes yellow," said the little girl.

"Yellow," said Mr. Rabbit. "You can't give her yellow."

"Something yellow, maybe," said the little girl.

"Oh, something yellow," said Mr. Rabbit.

"What is yellow?" said the little girl.

"Well," said Mr. Rabbit, "there are yellow taxicabs."

"I'm sure she doesn't want a taxicab," said the little girl.

"The sun is yellow," said Mr. Rabbit.

"But I can't give her the sun," said the little girl, "though I would if I could."

"A canary bird is yellow," said Mr. Rabbit.

"She likes birds in trees," the little girl said.

"That's right, you told me," said Mr. Rabbit. "Well, butter is yellow. Does she like butter?"

"We have butter," said the little girl.

"Bananas are yellow," said Mr. Rabbit.

"Oh, good. That's good," said the little girl. "She likes bananas. I need something else, though."

"What else does she like?" said Mr. Rabbit.

"She likes green," said the little girl.

"Green," said Mr. Rabbit. "You can't give her green."

"Something green, maybe," said the little girl.

"Emeralds," said the rabbit.
"Emeralds make a lovely gift."

"I can't afford an emerald," said the little girl.

"Parrots are green," said Mr. Rabbit,
"but she likes birds in trees."

"No," said the little girl, "parrots won't do."

"Peas and spinach," said Mr. Rabbit.
"Peas are green. Spinach is green."

"No," said the little girl. "We have those for dinner all the time."

"Caterpillars," said Mr. Rabbit.
"Some of them are very green."

"She doesn't care for caterpillars," the little girl said.

"How about pears?" said Mr. Rabbit. "Bartlett pears?"

"The very thing," said the little girl. "That's the very thing. Now I have apples and bananas and pears, but I need something else."

"What else does she like?" said Mr. Rabbit.

"She likes blue," the little girl said.

"Blue. You can't give her blue," said Mr. Rabbit.

"Something blue, maybe," said the little girl.

"Lakes are blue," said the rabbit.

"But I can't give her a lake, you know,"
said the little girl.

"Stars are blue."

"I can't give her stars," the little girl said, "but I would if I could."

"Sapphires make a lovely gift," said Mr. Rabbit.

"But I can't afford sapphires, either," said the little girl.

"Bluebirds are blue, but she likes birds in trees," said Mr. Rabbit.

"Right," said the little girl.

"How about blue grapes?" said Mr. Rabbit.

"Yes," said the little girl. "That is good, very good. She likes grapes. Now I have apples and pears and bananas and grapes."

"That makes a good gift," said Mr. Rabbit. "All you need now is a basket."

"I have a basket," said the little girl.

So she took her basket and she filled it with the green pears and the yellow bananas and the red apples and the blue grapes. It made a lovely present.

"Thank you for your help, Mr. Rabbit,"
said the little girl.

"Not at all," said Mr. Rabbit. "Very glad to help."

"Good-by, now," said the little girl.

"Good-by," said Mr. Rabbit, "and a happy birthday
and a happy basket of fruit to your mother."

Meet
Charlotte Zolotow

Charlotte Zolotow got the idea for *Mr. Rabbit and the Lovely Present* when her little girl was five years old. The author was sitting by an open window, and her daughter was outside. Suddenly, she heard the child say, "I don't know what to get my mother for her birthday." Then she heard an older person answer, "Why don't you pick her some flowers?"

That neighbor turned into Mr. Rabbit in Ms. Zolotow's story.

Meet
Maurice Sendak

Maurice Sendak says, "I'm very fond of *Mr. Rabbit and the Lovely Present.* The words tell a simple story, which my pictures had to show. But I was able to make the pictures tell another story of their own."

Mr. Sendak tells childen who want to be artists, "Make pictures that *you* like. Keep making them your own way."

KWANZAA

Our Family Picture Album

Kwanzaa is a holiday celebrated by some African Americans. It is celebrated for seven days, from December 26 to January 1.

We think about our past.
We celebrate our traditions.
We gather together and
learn more about our family.

We put ears of corn on the table.
The corn stands for children.
There is one ear of corn for each child.

We have a feast.
We eat foods of
our homeland.
We eat cornbread,
black-eyed peas,
and chicken.

We give one another
homemade gifts.
We make puppets.
We make pictures.

237

EZRA JACK KEATS

Ezra Jack Keats made the pictures in *A Letter to Amy* by painting over pieces of paper that he cut, tore, and pasted down.

Mr. Keats got the idea for Peter from some pictures of a child that he cut out of a newspaper. He had these pictures for 22 years before he made the first book with Peter in it. Other books by Ezra Jack Keats about Peter include *The Snowy Day, Whistle for Willie,* and *Peter's Chair.*

EZRA JACK KEATS

It is this Saturday at 2

A LETTER TO AMY

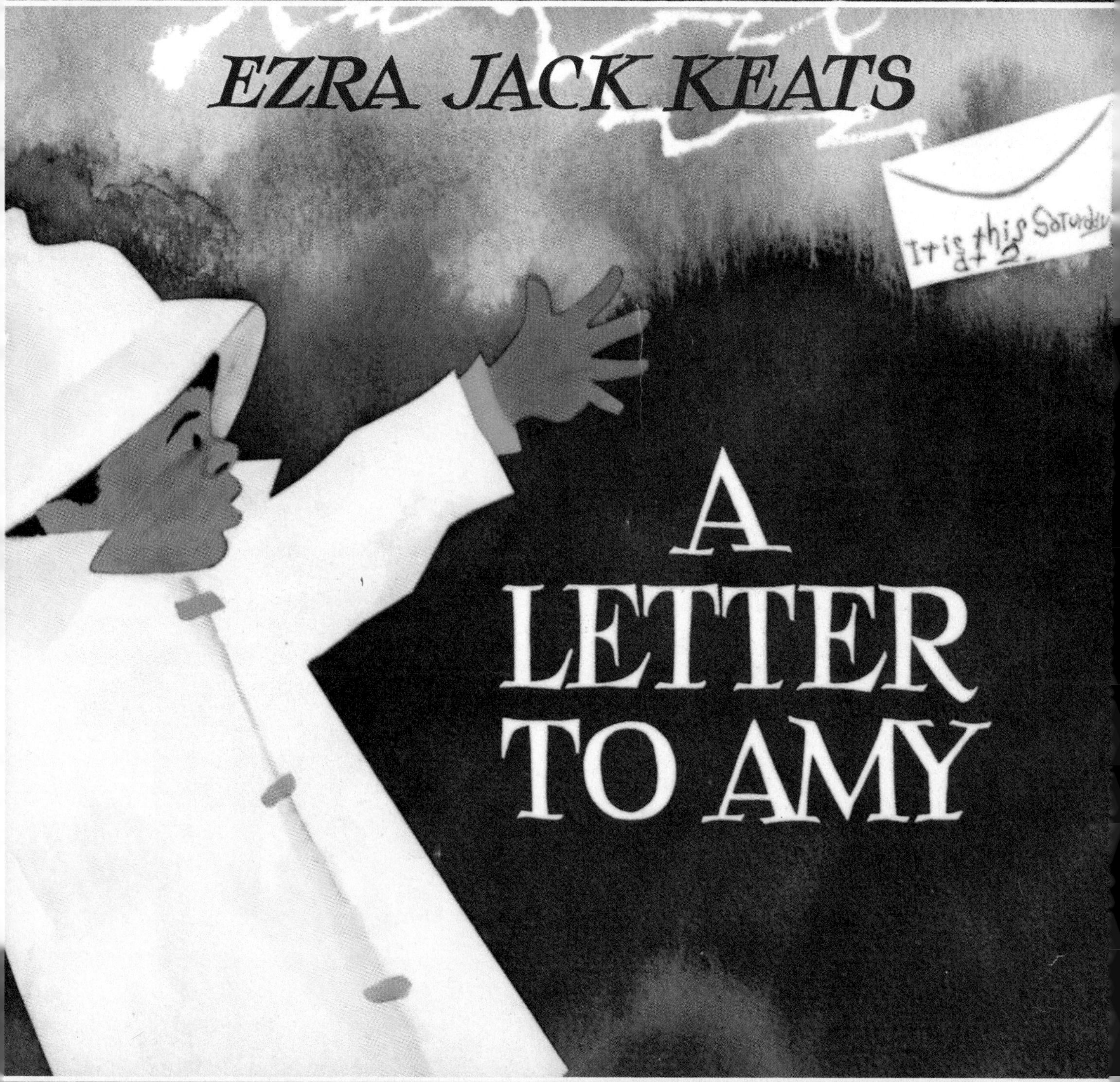

"I'm writing a letter to Amy.

I'm inviting her to my party," Peter announced.

"Why don't you just ask her? You didn't write to anyone else," said his mother.

Peter stared at the sheet of paper for a while and said, "We-e-el-l, this way it's sort of special."

He folded the letter quite a few times,
put it in the envelope, and sealed it.
"Now I'll mail it," he said.
"What did you write?" his mother asked.
WILL YOU PLEASE COME
TO MY BIRTHDAY PARTY. PETER.
"You should tell her when to come."
So he wrote on the back of the envelope:
IT IS THIS SATURDAY AT 2.
"Now I'll mail it."
"Put on a stamp."
He did, and started to leave.
"Wear your raincoat. It looks like rain."
He put it on and said, "It looks like rain.
You'd better stay in, Willie,"
and ran out to mail his letter.

Walking to the mailbox, Peter looked at the sky.
Dark clouds raced across it like wild horses.
He glanced up at Amy's window. She wasn't there.
Only Pepe, her parrot, sat peering down.
"Willie! Didn't I tell you to stay home?"

Peter thought, What will the boys say
when they see a girl at my party?
Suddenly there was a flash of lightning
and a roar of thunder!
A strong wind blew the letter out of his hand!

Peter chased the letter.
He tried to stop it with his foot, but it blew away.

Then it flew high into the air—

and landed, skipping across a hopscotch game.

The letter blew this way and that.
Peter chased it this way and that.
He couldn't catch it.

Big drops of rain began to fall.
Just then someone turned the corner.
It was Amy! She waved to him.
The letter flew right toward her.

She mustn't see it, or the surprise will be spoiled!
They both ran for the letter.

In his great hurry, Peter bumped into Amy.
He caught the letter before she could see it was for her.

Quickly he stuffed the letter into the mailbox.
He looked for Amy, but she had run off crying.

Now she'll never come to my party, thought Peter.
He saw his reflection in the street.
It looked all mixed up.

When Peter got back to his house, his mother asked, "Did you mail your letter?"
"Yes," he said sadly.

Saturday came at last.
Everybody arrived but Amy.

"Shall I bring the cake out now?" his mother asked Peter.

"Let's wait a little," said Peter.

"Now! Bring it out now!" chanted the boys.

"All right," said Peter slowly, "bring it out now."

Just then the door opened.
In walked Amy with her parrot!
"A girl—ugh!" said Eddie.

"Happy Birthday, Peter!" said Amy.
"HAAPPY BIRRRTHDAY, PEEETERRR!"
repeated the parrot.

Peter's mother brought in the cake she had baked
and lit the candles. Everyone sang.
"Make a wish!" cried Amy.
"Wish for a truck full of ice cream!" shouted Eddie.
"A store full of candy and no stomach-ache!"

But Peter made his own wish,
and blew out all the candles at once.

Celebra

I shall dance tonight.
When the dusk comes crawling,
There will be dancing
   and feasting.
I shall dance with the others
   in circles,
    in leaps,
     in stomps.
Laughter and talk
   will weave into the night,
Among the fires
   of my people.
Games will be played
And I shall be
   a part of it.

Alonzo Lopez

The Delight Makers, painted by Hopi artist Fred
Kabotie, shows clowns at a festival. This painting can
be seen in the National Museum of the American
Indian in New York City.

tion

INFORMATION ILLUSTRATED

A GUIDE TO SKILLS

AND INFORMATION

SOURCES

THAT GO

WITH THE

STORIES YOU

ARE READING!

CONTENTS

APRIL						
SUN	MON	TUE	WED	THUR	FRI	SAT
				1	2	3
4	5	6	7	8	9	10
11	12	13	14	15	16	17
18	19	20	21	22	23	24
25	26	27	28	29	30	

Apples Eaten in One Week	🍎 = 1 Apple
Mom	🍎🍎🍎🍎🍎
Dad	🍎🍎

1993

JANUARY

SUN	MON	TUE	WED	THUR	FRI	SAT
					1	2
3	4	5	6	7	8	9
10	11	12	13	14	15	16
17	18	19	20	21	22	23
24/31	25	26	27	28	29	30

FEBRUARY

SUN	MON	TUE	WED	THUR	FRI	SAT
	1	2	3	4	5	6
7	8	9	10	11	12	13
14	15	16	17	18	19	20
21	22	23	24	25	26	27
28						

MARCH

SUN	MON	TUE	WED	THUR	FRI	SAT
	1	2	3	4	5	6
7	8	9	10	11	12	13
14	15	16	17	18	19	20
21	22	23	24	25	26	27
28	29	30	31			

APRIL

SUN	MON	TUE	WED	THUR	FRI	SAT
				1	2	3
4	5	6	7	8	9	10
11	12	13	14	15	16	17
18	19	20	21	22	23	24
25	26	27	28	29	30	

MAY

SUN	MON	TUE	WED	THUR	FRI	SAT
						1
2	3	4	5	6	7	8
9	10	11	12	13	14	15
16	17	18	19	20	21	22
23/30	24/31	25	26	27	28	29

JUNE

SUN	MON	TUE	WED	THUR	FRI	SAT
		1	2	3	4	5
6	7	8	9	10	11	12
13	14	15	16	17	18	19
20	21	22	23	24	25	26
27	28	29	30			

JULY

SUN	MON	TUE	WED	THUR	FRI	SAT
				1	2	3
4	5	6	7	8	9	10
11	12	13	14	15	16	17
18	19	20	21	22	23	24
25	26	27	28	29	30	31

AUGUST

SUN	MON	TUE	WED	THUR	FRI	SAT
1	2	3	4	5	6	7
8	9	10	11	12	13	14
15	16	17	18	19	20	21
22	23	24	25	26	27	28
29	30	31				

SEPTEMBER

SUN	MON	TUE	WED	THUR	FRI	SAT
			1	2	3	4
5	6	7	8	9	10	11
12	13	14	15	16	17	18
19	20	21	22	23	24	25
26	27	28	29	30		

OCTOBER

SUN	MON	TUE	WED	THUR	FRI	SAT
					1	2
3	4	5	6	7	8	9
10	11	12	13	14	15	16
17	18	19	20	21	22	23
24/31	25	26	27	28	29	30

NOVEMBER

SUN	MON	TUE	WED	THUR	FRI	SAT
	1	2	3	4	5	6
7	8	9	10	11	12	13
14	15	16	17	18	19	20
21	22	23	24	25	26	27
28	29	30				

DECEMBER

SUN	MON	TUE	WED	THUR	FRI	SAT
			1	2	3	4
5	6	7	8	9	10	11
12	13	14	15	16	17	18
19	20	21	22	23	24	25
26	27	28	29	30	31	

CALENDAR

APRIL

SUN	MON	TUE	WED	THUR	FRI	SAT
				1 APRIL FOOLS' DAY	2	3
4	5	6	7	8	9	10
11	12	13	14	15	16	17
18	19	20	21	22	23	24
25	26	27	28	29	30	

DICTIONARY

bill

A **bill** is the hard part of a bird's mouth. **Bill** is another word for **beak**. ▲ **bills**.

biography

A **biography** is a true story of someone's life written by another person. ▲ **biographies**.

bird

A **bird** is an animal with wings. **Birds** are covered with feathers and have two legs. Most **birds** can fly. **Birds** lay eggs. Chickens, robins, and penguins are **birds**. ▲ **birds**.

birthday

Your **birthday** is the day and month when you were born. Keith and I have the same **birthday**. ▲ **birthdays**.

We sang "Happy Birthday" to Tommy on his **birthday**.

bite

1. Bite means to cut something with the teeth. The dog tried to **bite** the stick I threw her. Jesse **bit** into the apple.
▲ **bit, bitten** or **bit, biting**.
2. A **bite** is a piece you get when you **bite**. Jack took a **bite** of the banana. ▲ **bites**.

black

Black is a very dark color. These letters are **black**. The opposite of **black** is **white**.

blame

Blame means to say that a person has done something wrong or bad. Mother **blamed** me for letting the bird out of its cage.
▲ **blamed, blaming**.

Who took a **bite** out of Will's sandwich?

39

274

DICTIONARY

Our family **celebrated**
Grandma and Grandpa's
50th wedding anniversary.

celebrate
When you **celebrate** something,
you show that it is important in a
special way. Our town **celebrated**
the Fourth of July with a parade
and fireworks. ▲ **celebrated, celebrating.**

center
Center means middle. Cassie stood in the
center of the circle for the game. We put the
flowers in the **center** of the table. ▲ **centers.**

cereal
Cereal is a food often made from wheat,
corn, or rice. We like **cereal** for breakfast.
▲ **cereals.**

certain
Certain means that you are very sure about
something. Are you **certain** that you closed
the door?

chain
A **chain** is a row of rings that are joined
together. Margaret wore a heart on a **chain**
around her neck. ▲ **chains.**

chair
A **chair** is a piece of furniture with four legs
and a back. People sit on **chairs.** ▲ **chairs.**

Meg is using a **chain** to
keep her bike safe.

65

DIRECTIONS

WHAT?

A BIRTHDAY PARTY!

PLEASE COME

WHO: _Myra L._

WHEN: _May 16, 3 o'clock_

WHERE: _15 Oak Street_

Please reply _555 - 6145_

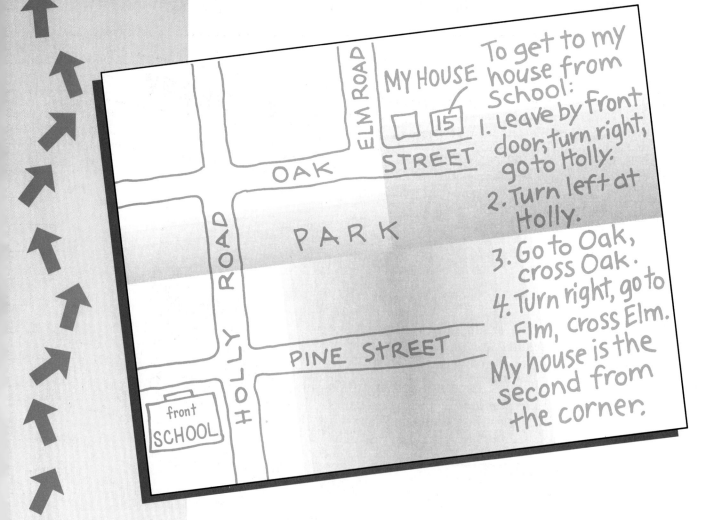

ELM ROAD

MY HOUSE

15

OAK   STREET

HOLLY ROAD

P A R K

PINE STREET

front
SCHOOL

To get to my house from school:
1. Leave by front door, turn right, go to Holly.
2. Turn left at Holly.
3. Go to Oak, cross Oak.
4. Turn right, go to Elm, cross Elm. My house is the second from the corner.

GRAPHS

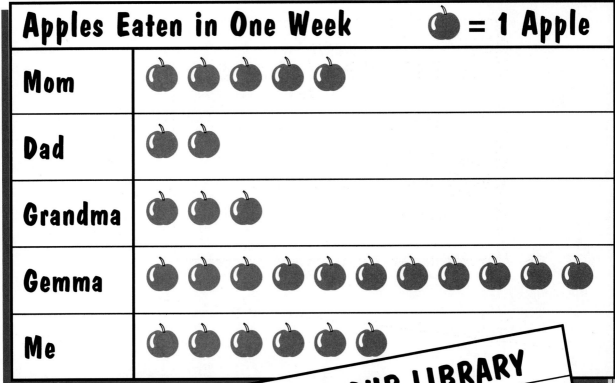

Apples Eaten in One Week	🍎 = 1 Apple
Mom	🍎 🍎 🍎 🍎 🍎
Dad	🍎 🍎
Grandma	🍎 🍎 🍎
Gemma	🍎 🍎 🍎 🍎 🍎 🍎 🍎 🍎 🍎 🍎 🍎
Me	🍎 🍎 🍎 🍎 🍎 🍎

ANIMAL BOOKS IN OUR LIBRARY

📘 = 1 Book

Birds   Cats   Dogs   Guinea Pigs   Horses   Snakes

Glos

This glossary can help you to find out the meanings of words in this book that you may not know.

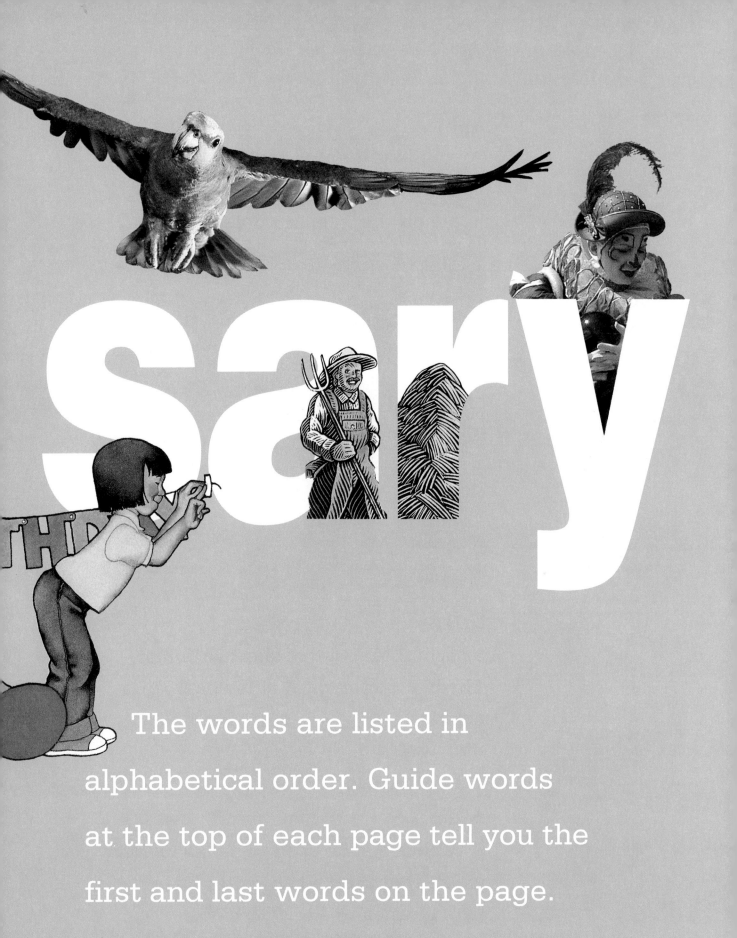

sary

The words are listed in alphabetical order. Guide words at the top of each page tell you the first and last words on the page.

apple

An **apple** is a round fruit with red, yellow, or green skin. We will pick an **apple** off the tree. ▲ **apples.**

bristly

Bristly means full of short, stiff hair. The hair on the back of my neck feels **bristly.**

cane

A **cane** is a stick used to help someone walk. Ned used a **cane** after he hurt his leg. ▲ **canes.**

caterpillar

A **caterpillar** is an insect that comes from an egg and then grows up to be a butterfly. A **caterpillar** looks like a worm with fur. ▲ **caterpillars.**

council

A **council** is a group of people called together to discuss a problem. The **council** met to talk about how to help the school get money for a new playground. ▲ **councils.**

decorate

Decorate means to make more beautiful. The children **decorate** the room for the birthday party. ▲ **decorated, decorating.**

elder

An **elder** is an older person who helps you decide what to do or how to do something. Sam learned much from his **elders**. ▲ **elders**.

explode

Explode means to break open suddenly and with a loud noise. Bright fireworks **explode** in the sky. ▲ **exploded, exploding**.

fancy

Fancy means special or fine. Amanda wore a **fancy** gown to the dance.
▲ **fancier, fanciest**.

feast

A **feast** is a large, special meal. We made a **feast** of different kinds of foods for Dad's birthday. ▲ **feasts.**

giant

Giant means very large. Whales and elephants are **giant** animals.

haystack

A **haystack** is a large pile of hay stored outdoors. The **haystack** is as tall as the farmer. ▲ **haystacks.**

invite

Invite means to ask someone to go somewhere. Alex sent Jill a card to **invite** her to his party. ▲ **invited, inviting.**

loan

Loan means to let someone have or use something for a while. Les will **loan** his bike to Louis. ▲ **loaned, loaning.**

mixture

A **mixture** is something made up of different things that are put together. The clown's coat is a **mixture** of many bright colors. ▲ **mixtures.**

parrot/piñata

P

parrot

A **parrot** is a kind of bird. Jan's **parrot** has green feathers. ▲ **parrots.**

piñata

A **piñata** is a colorful paper animal or other shape filled with candy or toys. It is usually hung from the ceiling and broken open with a stick. The birthday **piñata** looked like a donkey. ▲ **piñatas.**

285

R

rattlesnake

A **rattlesnake** is a kind of snake that has rings on its tail that rattle when it moves. ▲ **rattlesnakes.**

reflection

A **reflection** is what you see when you look in a mirror or in very shiny things. He saw his **reflection** in the window. ▲ **reflections.**

S

spicy

Spicy means full of spice. Spice adds flavor to food. The **spicy** food had too much pepper. ▲ **spicier, spiciest.**

T

treat

A **treat** is a nice, special thing. Maria gives her dog a **treat**. ▲ **treats.**

W

warn

Warn means to tell someone not to do something. Dan's mother will **warn** him not to cross the street when cars are coming. ▲ **warned, warning.**

INFORMATION ILLUSTRATED

DESIGN CREDITS

ILLUSTRATION CREDITS

PHOTOGRAPHY CREDITS